**The Impact of
Science and Technology**

COMMUNICATIONS

Andrew Solway

W
FRANKLIN WATTS
LONDON•SYDNEY

First published in 2009 by Franklin Watts

Copyright © 2009 Arcturus Publishing Limited

Franklin Watts
338 Euston Road
London NW1 3BH

Franklin Watts Australia
Level 17/207 Kent Street
Sydney, NSW 2000

Produced by Arcturus Publishing Limited
26/27 Bickels Yard
151-153 Bermondsey Street
London SE1 3HA

Series concept: Alex Woolf
Editor and picture researcher: Nicola Barber
Cover design: Phipps Design
Illustrator: Phipps Design (p15, 20 and 41)
Consultant: Bill Thompson

A CIP catalogue record for this book is available
from the British Library.

Dewey Decimal Classification Number: 302.2

ISBN 978 0 7496 9219 3

Printed in China

Franklin Watts is a division of Hachette
Children's Books, an Hachette UK company.
www.hachette.co.uk

CONTENTS

CHAPTER 1
Modern Communications 4

CHAPTER 2
Cables and Signals 8

CHAPTER 3
Radio 18

CHAPTER 4
Satellites 24

CHAPTER 5
Television 28

CHAPTER 6
The Internet 38

CHAPTER 7
Mobile Phones 48

CHAPTER 8
Looking to the Future 56

Glossary 60
Further Information 63
Index 64

Modern Communications

Teenager Rebecca Fyfe has good reason to be thankful for modern communications. When she and a group of friends found themselves drifting out of control on a damaged boat off the coast of Indonesia they were unable to contact local rescue services. So Rebecca texted her boyfriend, Nick, for help. Nick was in the United Kingdom – about 10,000km away! When he received her text he alerted the local coastguard, who got in touch with the rescue services in Indonesia. A ship was sent out, and eventually everyone was brought safely to shore.

Rebecca's text message was just one tiny part of the vast amount of information that we send across the world each day. Modern communication networks are so good that we almost take them for granted. The technology at the heart of all these networks is telecommunications.

Telecommunications

Telecommunication means 'communicating at a distance'. Any telecommunications system has the same basic parts. First, the information to be sent is turned into a signal. A transmitter then sends the signal through a transmission medium, such as a wire, to one or more receivers. The receiver picks up the signal and turns it back into information.

In the modern world there are all kinds of telecommunications systems. Whenever you make a phone call, listen to the radio, watch television or use the internet, you are using telecommunications. Police, firefighters and ambulance crews use two-way radio links to communicate during emergencies. Businesses rely on emails and telephone calls

VIEWPOINT

Good communication?

Advances in communications technology have not always met with universal approval:

'The more elaborate our means of communication, the less we communicate.'

(Joseph Priestley, eighteenth-century scientist and clergyman)

to correspond with their clients and each other. Banks rely on communications between computers to move money around the world.

✚ PROS: COMMUNICATIONS SYSTEMS

Good communication systems are an essential part of modern life, connecting people and businesses all over the world. Vast amounts of information can be transmitted instantly, and business transactions can be conducted in seconds. Today, it would be hard to imagine life without telephones, the internet, television or radio.

➖ CONS: COMMUNICATIONS SYSTEMS

Communications systems can sometimes provide people with too much information. Many people use the internet to search for a particular topic. But researching a popular subject on the internet can unearth far more information than it is possible to deal with. Looking up dinosaurs on Google, for example, produces links to over 20 million websites! Not all of these sites contain accurate information – and many of them simply sell products with a dinosaur theme.

Communications from the past

Before the development of modern tele-communications systems, people used many other forms of communication. Visual signals were made with fires, or mirrors that reflected light from the sun. Sound signals were made with drums, or with the human voice.

Printing made a huge difference to the communication of information. A German craftsman called Johannes Gutenberg developed a method of printing in about 1450, and within 50 years this technique had spread across Europe. At first, printers made books that only a few people could afford. Then, in the early 1500s, printers began to produce pamphlets. These cheap booklets were used to publish all kinds of information, ranging from the latest scientific discoveries to new religious ideas.

Whose invention?

It is often said that Johannes Gutenberg did not invent printing. In Korea, books had already been printed using individual bronze letters, and there were many kinds of ink before Gutenberg's time. But Gutenberg's printing process brought together lots of different ideas and improved on each one. His press applied pressure fast, so that pages could be printed quickly. He invented new metal alloys with the right properties for making type. And he developed new inks that worked well in his printing press.

➕ PROS: NEW TECHNOLOGIES

The improved communication that resulted from the development of printing had far-reaching effects. Many more books could be produced. They were still very expensive, but printers also produced short pamphlets and broadsheets that almost anyone could afford. Suddenly, people had access to information and new ideas as never before.

➖ CONS: NEW TECHNOLOGIES

New technology often leads to the loss of earlier forms of communication. The printing press, for example, replaced the skilled calligraphers and illuminators who created the beautiful handmade books of the Middle Ages. Similarly, the development of the internet and other electronic forms of information is threatening the existence of printed books and newspapers today.

Semaphore

In the early 1790s two French brothers, Claude and Ignace Chappe, developed what was perhaps the first real telecommunications technology – a signalling system called semaphore. The Chappes built a series of towers. On top of each tower was a long bar, with two shorter 'arms' that could be positioned in different ways to indicate different letters or words. Information could be passed rapidly along the line of towers from place to place. Semaphore spread across Europe and to the United States, although it was mainly used for military communications. By the 1830s it was being replaced by the electric telegraph.

One of the semaphore signalling towers designed in the 1790s by Claude and Ignace Chappe. A second tower can be seen in the distance, and the man on the right is reading its signal using a telescope.

CHAPTER 2

Cables and Signals

The electric telegraph is sometimes called the Victorian internet. Over a 100 years before the world wide web or communications satellites, the telegraph system was sending messages around the world. It was the earliest form of electric telecommunications.

The first successful electric telegraph was developed by two British inventors, William Cooke and Charles Wheatstone, in 1838. It used six wires and a set of five needles, each of which could be made to move left or right, to point to letters on a display. Although the needle telegraph was successful for a time in Britain, the equipment was complicated and expensive. It was soon replaced by an improved system from the United States. Samuel Morse and his assistant Alfred Vail invented a telegraph that used only one wire, and worked by sending messages in code. The code became known as Morse code,

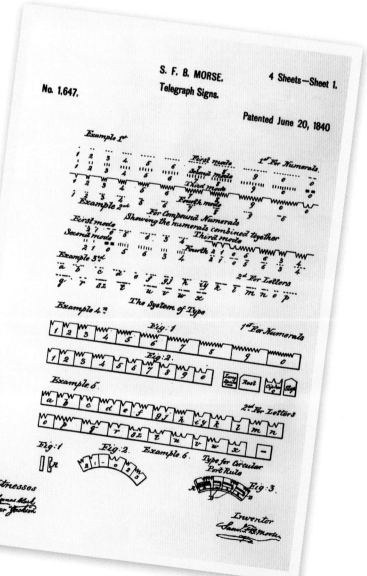

A patent gives inventors legal ownership of their inventions. This is part of the original patent documents for the Morse code. It shows the dots and dashes that make up the telegraph signs.

Morse code

Morse code translated each letter into a pattern of dots and dashes. These were sent using a telegraph key, which was simply a switch that sprang open when it was let go. The operator sent a dot by holding the key down very briefly, and a dash by holding it down slightly longer. At the other end of the wire, a printer recorded a black mark on a strip of paper whenever an electric pulse came through the wire. A dot was a short mark, while a dash was longer. Telegraph operators quickly learned to 'read' a Morse code message by listening to the pattern of clicks the telegraph made as a message came through. A skilled operator could send and receive messages very quickly.

although Vail developed it with Morse. The Morse telegraph was cheap and easy to use. The first Morse telegraph link was set up between Washington DC and Baltimore in 1844. Within a few years Morse's telegraph was being used in countries around the world.

A telegraph key for tapping out Morse code. Experienced operators could read a message from the sound of the taps, without having to look at the printout of the message.

Telegraph beats train

By the 1850s, most countries had a telegraph service of some kind. Newspaper reporters used the telegraph to send in their latest stories. The police found that it could be useful for catching criminals. In 1845 a woman called Sarah Hart was found dead from poisoning in her cottage in Slough, west of London. Suspicion soon fell on John Tawell, who had visited her that morning. The police learned that Tawell was on a train from Slough to London's Paddington Station. They telegraphed ahead to Paddington, and Tawell was arrested when he got off the train. It was the first time the telegraph had been used to catch a murderer.

Transatlantic links

In 1866 the SS *Great Eastern*, at that time the biggest ship in the world, laid a telegraph cable across the Atlantic Ocean. Soon there were connections between every continent. In 1885 over 33 million telegraph messages were sent, and by 1900 the number had risen to 90 million. The telephone was invented in 1876, and it soon replaced the telegraph for some communications. However, telegraph remained the only global communications network until 1927, when the first radio telephone link was made across the Atlantic (see page 16).

✚ PROS: ELECTRIC TELEGRAPH

The electric telegraph was very successful. The speed of communications provided by the telegraph made an enormous impact on society. Together with the railways, the telegraph forced a change to a faster-paced society.

➖ CONS: ELECTRIC TELEGRAPH

Telegraphs were limited in the information they could send. Until after 1900, most telegraphs used Morse code. This meant that skilled operators were needed to send and receive messages. Most people could not send their own telegraphs. The telegraph was also expensive. Only rich people and businesses could afford their own equipment; others had to use a public telegraph office. Private messages had to be sent using some kind of secret code.

"Mr Watson, come here…"

In March 1876, Alexander Graham Bell was trying out his latest design for a 'speaking telegraph'. He had been working on the idea for several years with his assistant, Thomas Watson. Speaking into the apparatus of his invention, Bell said to Watson, who was in another room, "Mr Watson, come here — I want to see you." This was the first telephone call. A new telecommunications revolution had begun.

The first few years of telephone history involved patent battles over who had the right to manufacture telephones. One of the large telegraph companies, Western Union, made telephones to the design of an American engineer called Elisha Gray. The American inventor Thomas Edison developed a microphone for the telephone that worked better than Bell's. There were more than 600 court cases challenging Bell as the inventor of the telephone. However, Bell's company won them all.

VIEWPOINT

An impractical device?

In 1876, Alexander Graham Bell and his financial backer, Gardiner Hubbard, offered the telephone patent to the Western Union telegraph company. This is part of the report of a committee who looked at the offer:

'Technically, we do not see that this device [the telephone] will be ever capable of sending recognizable speech over a distance of several miles … Furthermore, why would any person want to use this ungainly and impractical device when he can … have a clear written message sent to any large city in the United States?'

The first long-distance phone call was made by Alexander Graham Bell in 1892, from New York to Chicago.

Communicating through cables

The first telephones used a single steel wire, like the telegraph system. However, there was much more interference with the telephone signal than with a telegraph signal. Using two wires instead of one made some improvement. Another problem was that telephone signals could not travel far along steel wires. Experiments using different metals showed that signals travelled much farther in copper wires.

Even with the cables sorted out, there was still a problem with long-distance calls. The signal got gradually weaker and weaker. Then, in the early 1900s, the first amplifiers were developed. An amplifier is a device that boosts an electrical signal. By adding amplifiers at intervals, it became possible to send telephone signals thousands of kilometres.

How a telephone works

A telephone transmitter (the mouthpiece) turns sound into electrical signals, and the receiver (the earpiece) turns the signals back into sound. Thomas Edison invented the most widely used transmitter – the carbon microphone. Speaking into the microphone causes a thin metal plate, called a diaphragm, to vibrate. The vibrations of the plate produce a varying electric current – an electric signal. This signal is sent through the telephone wires to a receiver. The telephone receiver is a small loudspeaker. The changing electric current produces a changing magnetic field in a coil of wire. The coil pulls and pushes on another magnet, which is attached to a diaphragm. The pulls and pushes cause the diaphragm to vibrate, and these vibrations create sounds.

An early phone with a bell (top), mouthpiece (middle), and an earpiece (on the left-hand side). Early phones did not have an electricity supply. The caller turned the handle (on the right-hand side), which worked a small generator. This produced the electricity to power the phone.

Connecting people

An essential part of the telephone network was the telephone exchange. From the start, all the telephone lines from a local area were connected to a central exchange. In early exchanges, the calls were connected by human operators. This changed in 1889 with an invention made by an American funeral director called Almon Strowger. Strowger was convinced that an operator in his local exchange was putting through callers to a rival company. To stop this happening, he invented a system that connected calls automatically. Callers dialled a series of numbers, each of which sent electric pulses down the telephone line to the exchange. The electric pulses moved switches on a selector. Once the final number was dialled, the exchange connected the caller to the phone identified by that number.

A New York telephone exchange in 1897. By this date, millions of people had telephones. Each call had to be connected by hand, by an operator.

PROS: EARLY PHONES

In most ways, the telephone was a great improvement on the telegraph. For the first time, people could talk to each other directly over long distances. Although the telephone was expensive at first, it soon became cheaper. By 1900 there were over 3 million telephones in the United States alone.

CONS: EARLY PHONES

Early telephone systems were quiet, and the sound quality was especially poor over long distances. For many years telephone networks did not extend worldwide in the same way as the telegraph. A telephone call did not produce a written record. This meant that it was not useful for sending detailed information. For businesses in particular, the telephone was a useful addition, but it did not completely replace the telegraph.

Going digital

In 1937, a British engineer called Alex Reeves was looking for a way to cut out the background noise that plagued many telephone calls. Interference from other calls or from

Analogue and digital

The electrical signal produced by a telephone transmitter is continuously changing. Any electric signal that changes continuously is analogue. A digital signal is one that changes in sudden steps or jumps. This is because the signal is made up of thousands of 'samples' (measurements) of an analogue signal. Each sample has a specific value. For example, a signal might have a value of 2 at one point, and 4 a moment later.

To transmit a digital signal, each sample number is converted into a binary number. Binary is a numbering system that uses only the numbers 0 or 1. The number 2 becomes 10 in binary code, while 4 becomes 100. In this way, the analogue signal is turned into a long string of 1s and 0s. It can be transmitted as an electric signal with just two values.

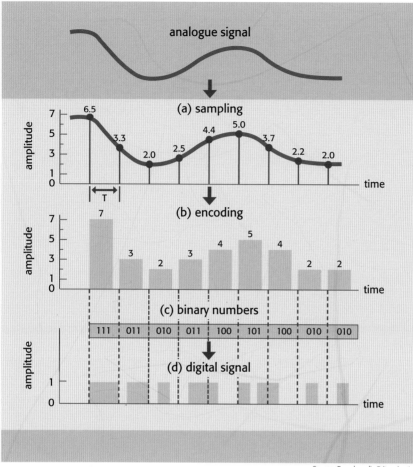

Turning an analogue signal into a digital one. The first stage is to sample the analogue signal (a). This means measuring it at regular intervals (T on the graph). The analogue signal is sampled many times per second. For conversion to a digital signal, the values for each sample are rounded up or down (b), then converted to binary numbers (c). These can be turned into a string of 'on' and 'off' pulses – a digital signal (d).

Source: Encyclopedia Britannica, Inc.

electrical equipment could cause all kinds of whistles, hisses and howls. He came up with the idea of turning the continuous electrical signal into a string of electric pulses. Reeves called his idea pulse-code modulation (PCM). Reeves's system turned an analogue telephone signal (one that changes smoothly and continuously) into a digital one.

A digital signal changes in small steps rather than continuously and can be 'written' as a string of binary code (using only the numbers 0 or 1). The great advantage of a digital signal is that because each point in the signal can have only value 0 or value 1, it is much easier to copy it exactly. Any 'noise' or interference has to be really serious before it can obscure the difference between a 0 or a 1. However, the first digital telephone exchanges were not set up until the 1970s, when microchips and computers made the technology easier and cheaper.

Fitting in more information

As telephones became more popular, it became difficult to provide enough lines for all the people who wanted to make calls. Engineers came up with several ways to send more than one call down the same line. One way of doing this with telephone calls is known as 'time-division multiplexing'. This involves breaking each telephone call into small sections, or 'packets'. A packet from one telephone call is sent down the line, then a packet from a second telephone call, and so on. The packets are joined up again at the other end of the line.

In the 1970s optical fibres added extra capacity to telephone lines. These thin, flexible strands of glass carry information using laser light rather than electricity. They can carry 65,000 times more information than a similar copper wire.

Optical fibres carry information as pulses of laser light. The light can travel huge distances along thin glass or plastic cables.

Telephone signals by radio

When radio was developed in the early 1900s (see page 19), it became possible to send telephone calls as radio signals rather than by wires. This worked best for long-distance calls that were difficult to make via cables, for example across an ocean. The first radio telephone call across the Atlantic Ocean was made between New York City and London on 7 January 1927.

⊕ PROS: TELEPHONE TECHNOLOGY

Improvements in telephone technology mean that you can now dial direct to anywhere in the world. The sound quality of intercontinental calls is almost as good as that of local calls. The low cost of long-distance calls has allowed some businesses to save money by locating their call centres in other countries where labour costs are lower. Call centres that deal with customers' questions are easy to 'outsource' in this way. Often people with questions about a Western company's product find their queries are answered by call centre staff in India.

⊖ CONS: TELEPHONE TECHNOLOGY

Telephone calls are often used as a way to sell products. Most people find such telemarketing very annoying. Telephone calls are also used to commit crimes. In one case, fraudsters in the United States phoned elderly people in the UK and persuaded them to buy shares in companies that turned out not to exist.

  Although the practice of outsourcing cuts costs for businesses, it is often not popular with their customers. Moving call centres away from the home country of a business can mean fewer jobs in that country. It can also lead to communication difficulties for people ringing the call centre.

Many companies have call centres, where people answer telephone calls from customers who have questions or complaints. Using modern communications, a call centre can be thousands of kilometres away from the customer. Many call centres for UK companies are in India.

CHAPTER 3

Radio

An old-fashioned name for a radio is a wireless. This name explains clearly the difference between early telephones and radios. Telephones needed wires to communicate, but radios did not. Instead, radio transmissions rely on radio waves, which are a type of electromagnetic radiation.

At first, radio was used to communicate between one person and another, like the telephone. Later, it was also used for broadcasting – sending out a radio signal that many people can receive at once. The first radio signals carried Morse code dots and dashes, but they quickly began to carry sound messages. Today a radio signal can carry a wide variety of communications – a text message, a telephone call, a TV programme or information from the internet, for example.

Electromagnetic radiation

Radio waves are one type of electromagnetic radiation, but there are many other kinds, each with a different wavelength and energy. Radio waves are long-wavelength, low-energy waves. At the other end of the scale are gamma rays and cosmic rays, which have very short wavelengths and high energy. All the different types of electromagnetic radiation move at the speed of light. Generally they travel in a straight line, but, like light, all electromagnetic waves can be reflected and refracted (bent).

Signalling with radio waves

Radio waves were first discovered in 1885 by the German physicist Heinrich Hertz. Hertz thought that these invisible waves would be of little use for communications. They travelled only a few metres, and if he placed the transmitters too close together they interfered with each other and just hissed. But within a few years of the discovery of radio waves, the Italian physicist Guglielmo Marconi had proved Hertz wrong. He developed a 'radio telegraph' that was like a Morse telegraph (see page 8), but without wires.

Marconi realized that radio was ideal for communications on the move. He persuaded several shipping companies to try out his radio equipment. In 1899 a coal ship called the *RF Matthews* crashed into the East Goodwin lightship off the coast of southeast England. The lightship was fitted with a radio and sent a distress message in Morse code to the shore. Lifeboats were sent to help in the first of many sea rescues made possible by radio communication.

In 1901 Guglielmo Marconi made history when he sent a radio signal across the Atlantic Ocean, from Cornwall, UK, to Newfoundland, Canada. This picture shows part of the powerful radio transmitter used by Marconi to send the signal.

The first broadcast

Meanwhile, a Canadian engineer called Reginald Fessenden was working on a radio system that could send continuous sounds. Fessenden produced a powerful wave, called a carrier wave. He added a sound signal to this carrier wave, and it was this combined signal that was transmitted. At the receiving end the carrier wave was separated from the sound signal, which was then played through headphones or a loudspeaker. This is the way that radio works today. Fessenden made the first radio broadcast on Christmas Eve 1906 from the coast of Massachusetts. The broadcast was heard by radio operators on ships far out to sea. A second broadcast on New Year's Eve reached as far as the West Indies.

Better radios

In 1906 an American inventor, Lee de Forest, invented a device called an Audion, or triode. It was a glass bulb, similar to a light bulb, that could be used to amplify radio signals, making them stronger. Before this, radio signals could only be heard through headphones. Now the amplified signal could power a loudspeaker.

During World War I (1914–18), governments in America and Europe banned private radio transmissions altogether. They wanted to keep the

AM and FM radio

Adding a sound signal to a carrier radio wave is known as modulation. In early radio, the sound signal modified the carrier wave by changing its amplitude (the size of each wave). This is called amplitude modulation, or AM. In 1935, an American engineer called Edwin Armstrong announced the invention of frequency modulation (FM). In FM, the sound signal changes the carrier wave's frequency (the number of waves produced per second). FM radio has the advantage that it is far less affected by interference than AM.

How (a) AM and (b) FM radio signals are formed. In AM radio, the sound signal (the modulating wave) changes the amplitude (height) of the carrier wave. In FM radio, the sound signal changes the frequency of the carrier wave (how far apart the waves are).

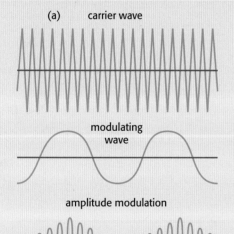
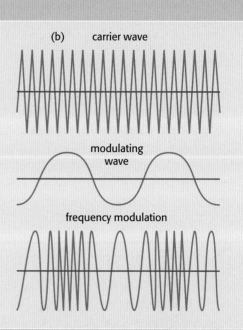

(a) carrier wave

modulating wave

amplitude modulation

(b) carrier wave

modulating wave

frequency modulation

Source: Computer Desktop Encyclopedia, 2007

airwaves free for vital military communications. For the first time, soldiers on the battlefields used radios to communicate with their commanders at headquarters. Soon after the war ended, national radio broadcasts began in both the United States and Europe.

Radios were used very differently in World War II (1939–45). By this time, most people had radios in their homes, so national broadcasts were used to keep people informed of what was happening. A new problem with military communications was the ability to tune into the enemy's radio messages. Important messages had to be coded to keep them secret. Soon both sides were busy breaking each other's codes, and an 'information war' began alongside the war on the ground.

Solid state electronics

After World War II, radios quickly got smaller. A new kind of amplifier called a transistor replaced the triode. Triodes were the size of light bulbs, whereas transistors were the size of peas. By the 1960s, transistor radios were cheap to buy and small enough to fit in a pocket. They were one of the reasons why rock and roll music became popular all over the world. Young people heard the music on the radio, then went out and bought their favourite records.

PROS: RADIO TECHNOLOGY

Radios do not require wires and poles to carry their signals. As a result, one of the first uses of radios was to communicate to and from places that weren't reachable by telephone, for example from ship to shore. Radios were soon also being used by the armed forces, police, ambulance and fire services, and for aircraft communications.

CONS: RADIO TECHNOLOGY

It is more difficult to keep radio signals free from interference than telephone signals. Radio transmissions can also be intercepted by anyone with the right equipment.

Separating signals

Many different carrier waves are used to transmit radio signals. These carrier waves each work at a different frequency, in order not to interfere with each other. The radio wave spectrum is divided into many different frequency ranges, called wavebands, each of which can carry a different signal. The size of a waveband (the bandwidth) depends on the amount of information it has to carry. A music radio station, for example, needs a large bandwidth.

In today's world, radio wavebands are very crowded. They are used to carry radio programmes, military radio, rescue service communications, TV signals, internet links – and even baby monitors. There are strict rules, made by the International Telecommunications Union, about which wavebands can be used for what purposes. Without these rules, television and radio broadcasts, phone calls, police radio and other transmissions would all interfere with each other and cause chaos.

Radio audiences

Before television, national radio stations had huge audiences. This was because there were few radio stations and no other competing media. Today many broadcasters are moving to digital broadcasts. Digital radio transmissions can be compressed, which makes it possible to have a large number of digital radio stations. However, this also means that each station has a relatively small audience. Different stations aim to attract different listeners.

VIEWPOINT

The importance of radio

In 2000, Sheila Patricka Dallas, general manager of United Nations Radio in Sierra Leone, explained why radio is such a vital technology:

'Radio is cheap to produce and to receive … There is some TV here in Freetown, but it doesn't reach the whole country. Radio can. In most places, electricity is erratic or even non-existent. Radios can be powered by batteries or even a hand-crank.'

Two disc jockeys (DJs) at work broadcasting from a radio studio in New York City, United States. Music radio stations, where DJs play music with short sections of news and chat, are extremely popular.

✚ PROS: RADIO BROADCASTS

There are many more radio stations than in the past, and this gives listeners more choice. This is especially true for music radio. FM and internet radio have high-quality sound, which is especially good for listening to music.

━ CONS: RADIO BROADCASTS

There are some problems with digital technology. Digital radios are more expensive, and they use more power than conventional radios. In addition, many areas cannot yet receive digital broadcasts.

CHAPTER 4

Satellites

In the late 1950s, humans travelled into space for the first time, sparking huge excitement around the world. However, other space launches that began at around the same time were also very important. These were satellites – small spacecraft that were launched into orbit around the Earth. Satellites play a very important part in modern communications.

By the 1950s the radio wave spectrum was becoming very crowded. There was not enough space for all the long-distance telephone calls that people wanted to make. One solution to the problem was to use satellites in space, which would act as mirrors to bounce radio waves back to Earth.

Communications satellites

The first successful satellite, the Russian *Sputnik 1*, was launched in 1957. It was not a communications satellite, but it broadcast radio signals for

A communications satellite pictured in orbit above Earth.

22 days as it orbited Earth. Two US satellites launched in 1960 were designed for radio communications. *Echo I* was a 'passive' satellite. It was a 30-m plastic balloon that simply acted as a mirror, reflecting radio waves back to Earth. *Courier 1B* was an 'active' satellite. It received radio signals, amplified them, then sent them back to Earth.

The first commercial communications satellite was *Telstar*, launched in 1962. As well as carrying telephone calls, it was used for long-distance television transmissions. More communications satellites soon followed, including another *Telstar* and three *Syncom* satellites. In 1964 the *Syncom 3* satellite was used to transmit live television coverage of the Tokyo Olympic Games across the Pacific Ocean from Japan to the United States.

Cameras film one of the first-ever satellite TV broadcasts, in 1961. In this broadcast, a speech by US President John F. Kennedy was beamed to the *Telstar* satellite in space, from where it was broadcast across Europe.

Building and launching communications satellites was expensive, but countries across the world could benefit. Satellite communications soon became a global business. In 1964, the International Telecommunications Satellite Organization (INTELSAT) was established. Eventually INTELSAT took over ownership of all satellites, and managed the global communications satellite network.

Satellite orbits

Satellites can be placed in many different types of orbit. With most orbits, transmitters and receivers on Earth need tracking devices to follow the movement of the satellite in the sky. There are also times when the satellite is out of contact. For this reason, communications satellites are often placed in geosynchronous orbit. This is an orbit in which the satellite travels round the Earth at the same speed as the Earth spins. Seen from the ground, the satellite seems to hover in the same spot.

Geosynchronous orbits are very high. Placing a satellite in such an orbit is expensive, and so are the satellites themselves. Satellites in low-Earth orbit (LEO) are much cheaper, because they can be smaller and less powerful. However, a whole array of LEO satellites is needed for continuous communications.

Other uses for satellites include television (see page 34) and mobile phones. Networks of LEO satellites make it easy to relay mobile phone calls over long distances. Satellite communications are now so good that news reporters send in broadcast-quality voice reports and videos from almost anywhere in the world, using a briefcase-sized transmitter that relays signals to a communications satellite.

➕ PROS: COMMUNICATIONS SATELLITES

Communications satellites have made communications truly global. In 1969, a string of satellites beamed live pictures of the first Moon landing to nearly every country in the world. Satellite TV has offered people much more choice. Satellite links can carry many more channels than Earth-based television broadcasts.

➖ CONS: COMMUNICATIONS SATELLITES

Satellites only work for a certain period of time. Once they stop working, they are simply space junk orbiting the Earth. There are now so many pieces of space junk that they are a hazard to space missions and to important unmanned spacecraft.

Communication by satellite makes it possible to get in touch from even the remotest places. This satellite telephone is on the trail to Mount Everest, nearly 4,000 metres above sea level.

Space junk

According to a report for the US space agency NASA, there are over 9,000 pieces of space junk orbiting the Earth. How dangerous are they?

'Only removal of existing large objects from orbit can prevent future problems … Although the risk is small, we need to pay attention to this environmental problem.'

(NASA report, 2006)

VIEWPOINT

CHAPTER 5

Television

A television set brings a whole range of information and entertainment directly into your home – films, dramas, news, chat shows, games and many other kinds of programme. Television was first developed in the 1920s and 1930s. By this time radio was very popular, and most homes had a radio set. It was also the period when the first 'talking movies' appeared. Television combined the two ideas of movies and radio broadcasts.

Inventing television

Several different people are said to have invented television. Probably the first demonstration of a complete television system was made by a British inventor called John Logie Baird, in 1926. Logie Baird used some ideas that had been developed earlier by other people. The most important part of his television was a spinning disc, invented in 1883 by a German, Paul Nipkow.

Logie Baird's television produced crude and fuzzy pictures. In 1923, when he was just 15 years old, an American student called Philo Farnsworth had an idea for a better system. He built the first demonstration model in 1929. Farnsworth's television was electronic – it had no mechanical moving parts. This meant that it produced much clearer pictures. However, it had the disadvantage that very bright lights were needed for the camera to get a good picture.

Transmitting pictures

Television signals contain far more information than a sound signal from the radio or a telephone. A television image is made up of more than 100,000 picture elements, or pixels (the 'dots' on the screen). Every second, 25 or 30 images are transmitted. This means that the picture signal has to be able to carry up to 3 million pieces of information every second. Sending this much information on a radio wave requires about 600 times more bandwidth than a radio signal.

The television system that was first widely used by television companies was developed by a Russian-born inventor called Vladimir Zworykin. In 1934, Zworykin developed a television camera called an iconoscope. It could produce pictures as good as those from Farnsworth's television system without the need for such bright lights.

Black and white

The first television companies formed in the 1930s. One of the first events to be televised was the Berlin Olympics, in 1936. At first, people did not have their own television sets. Instead, televisions were set up in theatres and in large stores, where many people could go to watch them. In the United States, television first attracted wide attention at a huge exhibition called the New York World's Fair, in 1939.

This blurred picture of a face is from what was probably the first ever public demonstration of television, by John Logie Baird in 1926.

Television becomes popular

After World War II, people in the United States began to buy television sets. In 1945 there were 7,000 TV sets in the whole country; by 1950 there were over 12 million. In Europe it took longer for television ownership to develop. Most people did not acquire television sets until the 1950s. In the UK, manufacturers rented televisions to make them more affordable.

The rise of television had a huge impact on movies and radio programmes. In the 1930s, cinema was hugely popular. Many people would go to the movies three times a week, or more. Films with news about recent events, called newsreels, were shown before main feature

A group of friends watch television together. In the United States, children and young people watch an average of 28 hours of television per week. In the UK, the figure is roughly the same for children 12 to 15 years old.

films. Once television became popular, the number of people going to the movies fell and newsreels disappeared. People could now watch the news several times a day on TV. Radio audiences fell, too.

Colour TV

John Logie Baird experimented with colour television as early as 1928, but colour television broadcasting actually began in the United States. After World War II, several US companies developed colour TV systems. However, it was not until the 1970s, when other countries apart from the United States also began to broadcast in colour, that colour TV really took off.

Cathode ray tubes

Until recently, cathode ray tubes (CRTs) were used for all televisions. A CRT is a large glass tube with no air inside. At one end are three electron guns. These fire streams of electrons along the tube (this is like a flow of electricity, because electricity is moving electrons). The electrons hit a screen at the other end of the CRT. This screen is covered with thousands of tiny dots of phosphor (a kind of chemical that lights up when electrons hit it). The phosphor dots are three different colours – red, blue and green. Each electron gun scans across the screen very fast, 'painting' the TV picture by lighting up phosphor dots. A new picture is 'painted' 25 or 30 times per second, so the eye sees a moving image.

➕ PROS: WATCHING TELEVISION

Television is a powerful way of getting information across because pictures have a more immediate impact than sounds or words. Studies by scientists show that television programmes can improve children's language and help their education.

➖ CONS: WATCHING TELEVISION

Television watching is a very passive activity. Many people get 'hooked': they sit in front of the television and watch whatever comes on the screen. Too much TV each day can mean that people do not get enough exercise. Some studies link the rise in the number of obese (overweight) people with television watching.

Recording television

In the 1940s and early 1950s there was no way of recording television programs and editing them. Anything that went wrong in a show simply went out live, sometimes with hilarious results. In one show, for example, an actor playing a character who had been shot and killed in the story crawled off the set while the live action continued around him.

Then, in 1956, a US recording company called Ampex produced the first experimental videotape recorders. These recorded programmes

A TV cameraman filming at a basketball game. In the past, high-quality television cameras were large and heavy. Today, professional quality television cameras can be hand-held.

directly on to magnetic tape. Until the late 1970s videotapes were stored and played on large open reels. In 1975, the Japanese company Sony introduced the first video cassette. Video cassettes used narrower tape, and the two tape reels were enclosed in a plastic casing. In the 1980s and 1990s, millions of people bought video cassettes to record television programmes.

At first, film and television companies fought against the introduction of videos. But they soon found that they could make large amounts of money from selling videos of films or programmes. Many movies were given new lives through sales of videos.

Video wars

The first video cassette recorders (VCRs) were produced by the Japanese firm Sony in 1975. The cassette system they used was called Betamax. In 1976 another Japanese company, JVC, produced a different home video system called VHS. The two video systems were not compatible. For several years there was a 'war' between the two companies to try and persuade the public to choose their system. In the end VHS became most popular, and Betamax disappeared. In the history of communications, there have been several 'wars' of this kind between competing versions of a new technology.

PROS: VIDEO RECORDING

Videotaping allows programmes to be edited before they are broadcast. Programmes can also be stored and shown again. Home video recording has made it possible for people to record their favourite TV programmes and watch them whenever they want.

CONS: VIDEO RECORDING

Because video footage can be edited, it is sometimes difficult to assess the accuracy of what is being shown. In 2007, there was a scandal in the UK when the trailer for a documentary about Queen Elizabeth II showed her walking angrily out of a photo shoot. In fact, the shot had been taken as she arrived at the photo shoot, not as she left. The way the footage had been edited gave the viewer an inaccurate impression of events.

Television through cables

Radio waves are ideal for broadcasting television. However, not everywhere is within reach of a television transmitter. Cable television began in the United States in the 1950s. It was used to reach remote areas where TV transmissions could not be received. People usually had to pay a monthly fee to receive television via cable. From the 1970s onwards, cable companies began to offer more TV channels. They could do this because cables can carry far more programmes than radio waves. Many people started to buy cable television for the extra channels.

Today, cable companies offer 24-hour news programmes, channels that show only movies, sports channels and many others. They also offer fast internet connections and cheap telephone calls.

Satellite TV

Satellite television is another system that offers many channels to viewers. Satellite TV broadcasts are carried by microwaves, which can carry more channels than radio waves. Because communications satellites orbit high above the Earth, their transmissions reach a large area. Satellite companies charge customers for the channels that they supply. To stop anyone with a satellite dish from being able to pick up their

LCD stands for liquid crystal display. LCDs are one of several kinds of flat screen that have replaced CRTs as television screens. The 274-cm screen shown here is one of the biggest.

108" WORLD'S LARGEST LCD TV

AQUOS

broadcasts, the television signals are encoded (scrambled). People who pay for a particular satellite service are given a decoder (unscrambler).

➕ PROS: CABLE AND SATELLITE

In the early days of television, cable channels gave a better-quality picture than channels received with a signal from a transmitter. Today, both cable and satellite television offer viewers a far greater choice of channels than ever before. Customers may also get other benefits such as cheap, high-speed internet connections.

➖ CONS: CABLE AND SATELLITE

The need to fill airtime on the large number of channels on satellite and cable networks has resulted in the questionable quality of many of the programmes shown. For example, there are many shopping channels, which simply advertise products and offer them for sale.

Television: good or bad?

VIEWPOINT

Experts disagree about the effects that TV has had on people's lives:

'Adolescents who watched more than one hour a day of television … were roughly four times more likely to commit aggressive acts toward other people later in their lives than those who watched less than one hour.'

(Results of a study led by Prof. Jeffrey Johnson of Columbia University, New York)

'At its best, TV can educate and inspire. High-quality documentaries offer insights into history that no book can equal. Nature programmes take us to places many of us will never be able to visit …'

(From the book The Elephant in the Living Room by Dimitri Christakis and Fred Zimmerman, experts in television and child development)

Going digital

As computers have developed and become increasingly important, various parts of the television process have been digitized. In television cameras, charge-coupled devices (CCDs) record the brightness patterns of a scene as millions of individual pixels, rather than as a continuously changing signal. Digital processors turn the raw picture and sound information into a television signal. Optical discs such as DVDs store video signals digitally, and can be used to play them back. The flat LCD and plasma displays that have replaced CRTs also work digitally.

In the early twenty-first century, cable and satellite companies began to broadcast some programmes digitally. A digital television signal can be compressed before it is transmitted, so a digital signal takes up less bandwidth than an analogue one. This means that more channels can be broadcast. There is also space for interactive TV, where viewers can send messages or choose what they watch.

However, most of the major television broadcasters still broadcast analogue programmes. This is because millions of television viewers have television sets that cannot receive digital signals. Most of the more developed countries will change over completely to digital broadcasts in the near future. Countries in the European Union will complete the switchover by 2012. In the United States switchover to digital TV will be completed by 2009, in Japan by 2011 and in Australia by 2013.

➕ PROS: DIGITAL TV

Digital televisions give better sound and picture quality. Each digital channel also takes up less bandwidth, so more channels can be transmitted. This gives viewers more choice.

➖ CONS: DIGITAL TV

The switchover to digital TV will mean that analogue television sets will not work without modification. Anyone who wants to receive digital TV will either have to buy a new television, or get a digital box.

HDTV

Since the 1960s, the pictures on our television screens have been made up of either 525 or 625 lines. However, digital signals can carry more information in the same bandwidth, so digital transmissions can be better quality. Some TV programmes are now made in high definition (HD). These HD images are almost ten times more detailed than normal television pictures. Some satellite and cable television broadcasts are already HD. There are also many HDTV sets now on sale (usually large plasma screens). However, until there is a complete digital switchover, many programmes will still be SDTV (standard definition television) broadcasts.

The CBS3 television news studio in Philadelphia, Pennsylvania, United States, was one of the first to produce all its broadcasts in high definition.

CHAPTER 6

The Internet

The internet has had a bigger impact on communications than anything since printing. Most people only began to be aware of the internet in the 1990s. But it began in the 1960s, when a group of scientists tried to tackle the problem of getting different computers to talk to each other.

The first networks

In 1960 the American computer scientist Joseph Licklider put forward the idea that computers could one day be connected through a world network of high-speed links. In 1962 Licklider went to work for the US Department of Defense Advanced Research Projects Agency (DARPA). He set up a group to find ways of sending information between different computers. In 1969 the group connected four computers at different research centres in the United States. This network, called the Advanced Research Projects Agency Network (ARPANET), was the first step on the road to the internet.

Information packets

The crucial technology at the centre of the ARPANET was something called packet switching. This was a way of sending information from one computer in a network to another. Packet switching has important advantages over other ways of sending information. Because each packet is short, the connection between one point in a network and another only has

Packet switching

In packet switching, a piece of information being sent through a network is chopped up into small pieces, or packets. Each packet has a 'label' on it saying where it is from, where it is going, and where the packet fits into the overall piece of information. The packets are sent separately through the network. At each connection in the network there is a computer called a router, whose job is simply to send on packets from one place to the next. Different packets may take different routes from sender to receiver. The packets are put back in the right order as they arrive at their final address.

to be open for a short time for the packet to travel along it. A break in communication does not mean that the whole message has to be sent again. Another advantage of breaking information up is that packets can travel by different routes, and packets from many different messages can use the network at the same time.

Connecting networks

The ARPANET soon added more computer centres to its network. Other groups also set up their own networks using the packet switching idea. By the early 1970s there were several networks, all working independently of each other. Connecting these networks together was a problem, because the computers used different systems for talking to each other. Robert E. Kahn at DARPA and Vinton Cerf of Stanford University came up with an idea to solve this problem. They suggested that whatever system was used within a network, when networks communicated with each other they would use a common set of rules. Kahn, Cerf and others developed a protocol (set of rules) called TCP/IP. It became the common language of the internet in 1983, and it is still used today.

Friends meet at an internet café. Today, the internet is part of everyday life for vast numbers of people around the world.

You've got mail!

Email was one of the first ways the internet was used, and is still one of the most popular. Email was used before the internet began to develop commercially in the 1990s, but only in a very limited way. In 1972 Ray Tomlinson, who worked on the ARPANET, came up with the email address format that we still use today: 'sender@address'. Today there are about 1.3 billion email users worldwide, and nearly 2.5 million emails are sent on the internet every second.

How emails work

Most individuals are connected to the internet through their internet service provider (ISP). A server (a large, fast computer) at the ISP has a 'postbox' for each person's email. When you send an email to a friend, it goes first to your postbox, then travels through the internet to your friend's postbox. To pick up the message, your friend connects to their postbox on the ISP server, and looks in their inbox. They can either read the emails without moving them from the postbox, or download the emails to their own computer.

➕ PROS: EMAIL

Emails were probably the biggest benefit of the early internet. Email has two advantages over the telephone. First, you don't have to look at an email as soon as it arrives – you can choose your own time. Second, emails are written. This means that they can be used to send complex information, such as facts and figures.

➖ CONS: EMAIL

The biggest problem with email is spam – unwanted emails that are sent to thousands or millions of people at once. Over 70 percent of all email traffic is spam. Some is advertising, and is simply annoying. However, other spam emails contain viruses or other programs that can damage a computer or steal personal information such as bank details.

Instant messaging

Instant messaging was first used in the 1960s, but it did not become a common part of the internet until the mid-1990s. When someone logs on to their instant messaging service, they can see which of their friends or contacts are also online. They can send a text message to any of these people, and it will appear immediately on the other person's computer screen. The two people can continue to chat online, with messages appearing on the screen as they are typed. Some instant messaging providers also offer extra features such as group chatting or online conferencing using sound and video.

In instant messaging, two people can have a real-time 'conversation' just as if they were on the telephone – except the conversation is through writing instead of talking.

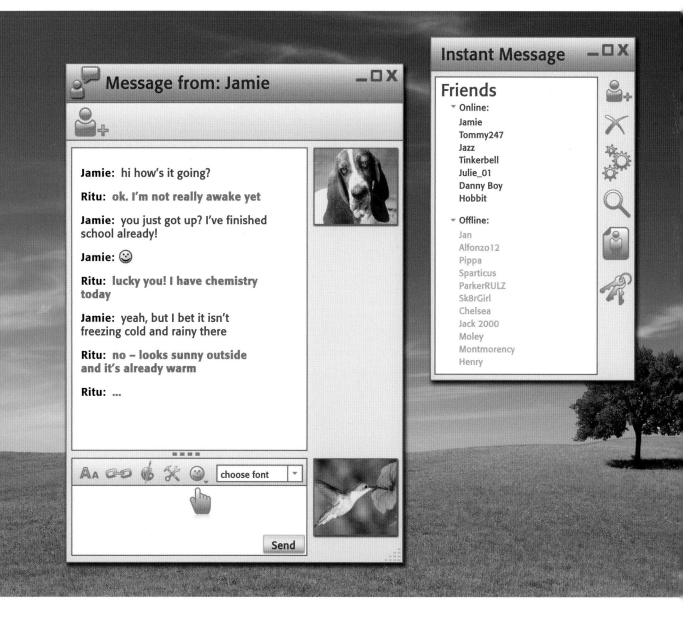

Changing use

In the 1970s the invention of microprocessors made it possible to build smaller, cheaper computers. By the late 1970s people were beginning to buy personal computers (PCs) to use either for work or at home. When PCs first appeared, using the internet involved writing computer commands. It was not at all user-friendly. But in the late 1980s and early 1990s the internet became much more accessible to ordinary people.

The world wide web

The main way most people use the internet today is to get to the world wide web, the vast collection of websites and pages that are visible online. The idea of the web was developed at the European Organization for Nuclear Research (CERN) by an English scientist, Tim Berners-Lee. He invented hypertext, a way of linking one piece of information to another on the internet by clicking on a word or picture. Berners-Lee built all the tools needed to create web pages, and in 1991 he put up a notice on the internet explaining about the world wide web and inviting other people to become involved. This was the first ever web page.

With the development of the world wide web, the internet became much more user-friendly. In the early 1990s, the internet began to turn into a commercial network and the first internet service providers (ISPs) appeared. Web browsers such as Mosaic made it easier for people to use the network, and search engines such as Yahoo!, AltaVista and Google helped users to find material.

VIEWPOINT

Internet: good or bad?

This summary of the advantages and the drawbacks of the internet comes from an essay written in 2000 by Bill Gates, then head of the Microsoft Corporation:

'Some optimists view the internet as humanity's greatest invention … At the other extreme, pessimists think the internet will result in … the death of privacy, and a decline in values and social standards. If history is any guide, neither side of these arguments will be proved right.'

PROS: INTERNET

Scientific researchers were using the internet to share ideas and results long before it became popular. As more people connected to the internet, everyone from journalists to schoolchildren began to use the internet to find out things they wanted to know.

CONS: INTERNET

Information from the internet is not always reliable. Some websites have information that is inaccurate. Others give only one side of an argument, or even information that is deliberately false.

The Google search engine was launched on the internet in 1998. It quickly became popular for its ability to give relevant search results. Today Google is far more than just a search engine. In 2007, the company launched Google Sky – a virtual telescope that allows internet users to view 100 million stars and 200 million galaxies.

Boom and bust

The number of computers connected to the internet grew rapidly in the 1990s. In 1990 there were about 300,000. By 1999 this number had risen to over 56 million. Until the mid-1990s, the internet was run by universities and research organizations. These organizations did not allow the internet to be used for making money. But from about 1994, commercial companies began to take over the internet.

Hundreds of new internet companies sprang up. At first these 'dot-com' companies were very successful. However, making money on the internet turned out to be no easier than making money in any other business. In 2000 the dot-com industry collapsed, and many companies went bust. Some dot-com companies, such as Google, eBay and Amazon, survived the collapse and went on to become large businesses. New dot-com companies such as YouTube and Facebook have also developed since 2000, and have had great success. Millions of other businesses use the internet as a way of advertising and selling their products and services.

Access to the internet

VIEWPOINT

The internet is increasingly important – but large numbers of people do not have access to such technology. People in richer countries have more opportunities to use the internet than people in poorer ones:

'The importance of the internet in a teenager's life increases with every day that goes by. Teenagers are starting to use the internet in a myriad of ways, which range from doing schoolwork to transporting themselves halfway around the world ...'
(David Thelen, US high-school student)

'Globalization, as defined by rich people like us, is a very nice thing ... you are talking about the internet, you are talking about cell [mobile] phones, you are talking about computers. This doesn't affect two-thirds of the people of the world.'
(Former US president Jimmy Carter)

Making the world smaller

The end of the dot-com boom did not stop the growth of the internet. In 2008 there were nearly 600 million computers connected to the internet, and a total of nearly 1.5 billion internet users. This is almost a quarter of the world's total population.

You can do a huge range of things on today's internet. For example, you can listen to music or watch television, play games with a group of friends, go shopping, book a holiday, get tickets for a concert or take a virtual trip around the world. The internet can also be used in more serious ways. People in some businesses work from home for clients anywhere in the world. People campaigning against injustice can make their voice heard in many places. People with a medical problem can get in touch with others who have the same illness to share support and information. Many people pay their bills, and manage their bank accounts and other household services online. On top of all this, there is information on the internet on every subject imaginable – all available at the click of a mouse.

Fans of the British rock group the Arctic Monkeys made a MySpace website where people could hear their music. The site helped make the band very popular even before they had released a record.

TV and wireless

The most recent development in internet communications is wireless connection. This involves using high-frequency radio signals to send information to and from a receiver connected to the internet. Wireless links can be used in homes and offices to connect a group of computers to the internet. There are also 'hotspots' in many towns and cities, where any computer with a wireless link can connect to the internet. More recently, it has become possible for a computer to use a mobile phone as a direct connection to the internet.

Grid computing

The internet is a great way to share information across the world. But single computers do not have enough memory or processing power for some jobs. So scientists are turning to a new kind of network, called grid computing. Computers on a grid interconnect to share memory and processing power, turning them into one vast, powerful mega-computer. An example of grid computing is the WISDOM project, which began in 2005. This medical project has been using grid computing to look at the structures of 1 million chemicals, to see if any might make good anti-malarial drugs. In just three weeks, the list of chemicals was reduced to 30 likely candidates.

These computers at CERN in Switzerland are part of a grid network that allows CERN to share information with scientists around the world.

⊕ PROS: GLOBAL COMMUNICATIONS

The internet has given many people a voice. For example, when the United States and its allies invaded Iraq in 2003, a blogger in Baghdad, called Salam Pax, wrote about the war from an Iraqi point of view. In September 2007, news of mass protests in Burma reached the rest of the world through photos and short videos sent over the internet by people in Burma.

⊖ CONS: GLOBAL COMMUNICATIONS

The internet has created opportunities for many new kinds of crime. A common crime is identity fraud. Criminals find ways of getting internet access to information such as a person's address, telephone number, date of birth and bank information. They then pretend to be that person and defraud them. Some internet criminals target young people. They join chat lines or social networks and pretend to make friends. They actually want to do harm. All young people using the internet need to be aware of the dangers from such people.

Safety rules on the internet

- Do not give out your home address, phone number or school.
- Do not arrange to meet someone you know only online, or send them your picture.
- People do not always tell the truth on the internet and are not always who they seem.
- Always tell parents or teachers if you get nasty messages.

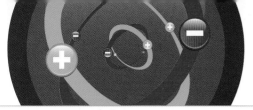

CHAPTER 7

Mobile Phones

Mobile phones became hugely popular in the 1990s. However, mobile phone technology has been developing slowly since the 1920s. Probably the earliest 'mobile' telephones were installed in 1926 on passenger trains in Germany. By the 1950s, a few radio telephones were being used in cars. These early mobile phones worked by sending out a strong radio signal to a central radio transceiver (a combined transmitter and receiver), which picked up the signals and sent them on through the normal telephone system. The phones were large and heavy, and needed powerful batteries.

A major problem with early radio phones was that very few could be used in a particular area. This was because only a small part of the total radio wave spectrum could be used for radio telephones without interfering with other radio transmissions.

The cellular idea

The breakthrough idea that eventually led to modern mobiles came from two engineers at Bell Laboratories in the United States in 1947. Douglas Ring and Rae Young came up with a way for a large number of phones to communicate with the telephone system using only a small number of radio channels. Their idea was for a network of radio transceivers, each of which would pick up and send signals within a fairly small area, called a 'cell'. Each cell was six-sided. This hexagonal shape works best because the cells fit together neatly, like the cells in a honeycomb. Each transceiver sent and received messages only over the area of its cell. When a phone reached the edge of a particular cell, the call would be handed over to the next cell. Rae and Young worked out that they could avoid interference between cells using just seven different radio channels. These seven channels could be used in a repeating pattern over a large area.

Walkie-talkies

During World War II, armed forces developed fairly lightweight two-way radio sets that became known as walkie-talkies. The first US walkie-talkie was a device called the Handie-Talkie. It weighed about 2.3kg and was about 35cm long. English engineer Donald Hings developed a slightly bigger walkie-talkie for the British and Canadian armies in about 1941. The intensive research work that went into walkie-talkies contributed to the development of mobile phone technology.

A police officer in Hong Kong uses a modern walkie-talkie to communicate with colleagues.

The first cellphone

When Ring and Young came up with the cellular idea, the technology to make it work was not available. Keeping track of many different mobile phones, and 'handing over' each one as it moved out of one cell and into the next, required the processing power of a computer. However, the few computers that existed in 1946 were room-sized.

The development of transistors and computers after World War II meant that by the 1960s cellular technology was possible. In 1970 Amos Joel, another engineer at Bell Laboratories, developed a method for automatically handing over a phone call from one cell in the network to another. In 1973 Martin Cooper, an engineer at the US company Motorola, demonstrated the first truly mobile cellular phone.

Battery technology

A large part of the weight and size of early mobile phones was due to the battery. Many early handsets had a separate battery pack. In the 1990s new batteries were made with a combination of nickel and a metal alloy. These small nickel-metal hydride (NiMH) batteries provided plenty of power. Modern mobiles use even smaller batteries, made from the metal lithium. The latest lithium polymer batteries are very slim and can be shaped to fit the phone casing.

Setting up networks

US scientists were the first to develop cellular technology. However, when it came to setting up cellular networks, other countries were ahead of the United States. The first commercial mobile phone network was launched in Tokyo, Japan, in 1979. In 1981 the Nordic Mobile Telephone system, which covered Finland, Denmark, Norway and Sweden, began operating. By 1985 more than 200,000 people were using that network, making it the biggest in the world at the time.

PROS: EARLY MOBILES

Although early mobile phones had their limitations, they showed that mobile technology could work. Mobiles were especially useful in places such as Scandinavia, where there are few people spread over a large area, and laying telephone cables to every home is expensive.

CONS: EARLY MOBILES

Early mobile phones were large and heavy, and expensive. The first commercial Motorola phone weighed over 450g and cost US$3,500. Early phones also had a very short battery life – perhaps only having enough power for ten minutes of continuous talk time.

Second generation

Mobile phone technology improved very quickly. In the early 1990s new digital networks were set up that were a great improvement on the earlier analogue networks. A second generation of mobile phones began to appear that were smaller, lighter and cheaper than the earlier 'bricks'. They had a screen, a telephone directory and some simple games. With these improvements, the mobile phone suddenly mushroomed in popularity, especially in Japan and the UK.

Around the world, antennae like this one pick up microwave signals from mobile phones and feed them into the conventional telephone network.

Txt msgs

One of the biggest surprises of the second-generation phone systems was the success of text messaging. GSM, which was the phone system set up in Europe, included a feature called the short messaging service (SMS). This allowed phone users to send brief text messages with fewer than 160 characters. To keep to this limit, people shortened words and phrases, or replaced them with symbols.

PROS: TEXTING

Text messages are simple to send. They are cheaper than a phone call, and the person receiving the text can respond in their own time.

CONS: TEXTING

Text messaging can become addictive, and can stop people from learning or working effectively. Many accidents have been caused by people texting while driving.

A Google T-Mobile G1 phone (left) and an Apple iPhone (right). Modern phones like these are some of the most sophisticated electronic devices in the world.

The dangers of mobile phones

After many years of research into the safety of mobile phones, some experts believe they pose little or no danger to human health, while others take the opposite view:

'Mobile phones, cordless phones and cordless base stations next to beds are safe, pose no risk of cancer to adult users and do not cause headaches or sleeping problems.'

(Report in the British Medical Journal, 2008)

'Children and teenagers are five times more likely to get brain cancer if they use mobile phones, startling new research indicates.'

(Swedish research report, 2008)

3G

In the twenty-first century, mobile networks have changed once again. Third-generation (3G) phone networks offer far more than just phone calls. The phone signals are greatly compressed, which leaves space to use some bandwidth for other purposes. People can send and receive emails, surf the internet, and even watch streaming videos on their mobile phone. 3G phones also have many more features, such as a colour screen, an MP3 player, a camera and sometimes a GPS system (a satellite navigation system that allows you to know your position anywhere on Earth). Some mobiles have a keyboard rather than just a number pad. These 'smartphones' are mini-computers as well as phones.

⊕ PROS: MOBILE PHONES

Mobile phones have became an essential part of many people's lives. In emergency situations, mobiles have frequently made it possible to call for help. For example, in 2007 three climbers who fell on Mount Hood in Oregon, United States, were rescued when other climbers with them used their mobiles to alert the rescue services.

CONS: MOBILE PHONES

Mobile phones are very useful, but it is important to know when to turn them off. Business people often feel that they must keep their mobile phones on all the time. However, always being available to receive calls can make people very stressed. The ring tones of mobile phones, and overhearing other people's phone conversations, can cause annoyance and distraction to others in places such as theatres or trains. Mobile phones may be a health risk. For example, some scientific studies suggest that using mobile phones for several years can increase the risk of getting brain or ear cancers. However, other scientific studies show no health risks from mobile phones.

An X-ray of a mobile phone shows the complex electronic circuits inside.

What's inside a mobile?

A mobile phone packs an enormous amount of technology into a small space. Like a conventional telephone, the mobile needs a microphone and a speaker. It also needs a battery, an aerial to pick up radio signals and a screen to display information. However, the most important parts of the phone are the electronics. There are several different electronic parts:

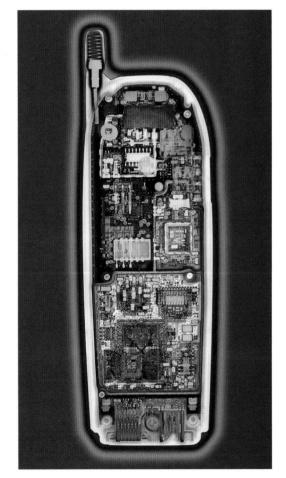

- **Analogue to digital (A to D) microchips** The signals coming from the microphone and going to the speakers are analogue, but the signals transmitted and received are digital. A to D microchips convert the signals back and forth.
- **Digital signal processor (DSP)** The signals going in and out from the phone are highly compressed. The DSP does the compressing and decompressing.
- **RF (radio frequency) chips** These produce the radio waves that carry the phone signals. An amplifier chip makes the signals stronger.

- **Memory chips** The memory is used to store phone numbers and other information.
- **Microprocessor** The microprocessor is the 'brains' of the phone. It broadcasts the phone's unique identity number, so that the system knows where the phone is. The microprocessor also knows the radio frequencies of the nearest cells, and monitors the strongest signal at each moment.

PROS: MOBILE REVOLUTION

The mobile phone brings together most of the modern communications media, including radio, television, email and the world wide web. Many mobiles can be used to record sounds and music, take pictures and make short videos.

CONS: MOBILE REVOLUTION

Although mobile phones are expensive, they do not last long. Manufacturers are always bringing out new phones with more features. The result is that billions of phones are thrown away each year. Phones form a significant part of the millions of tonnes of electronic waste (e-waste) thrown away each year – around 50 million tonnes globally.

Environmental impact

VIEWPOINT

In 2006, Dr Dylan Gwyn Jones of the University of Wales researched the environmental impact of mobile phones.

'As with all electronic equipment, mobile phones contain a range of substances that are harmful if the devices are not disposed of properly. Heavy metals such as mercury, lead and cadmium are present within mobile phones, especially older models …'

CHAPTER 8

Looking to the Future

In this book we have examined the various different kinds of communications technology separately, but all these technologies are interconnected. The first telephones used telegraph wires to send signals. Television broadcasts are transmitted using radio waves. Home computers connect to the internet through the telephone network.

Mobile phones are the essence of modern communications. A modern mobile phone can replace nearly all other modern communications devices. You can use it as a telephone, a radio and a music centre. You can surf the internet and you can find your location using the Global Positioning System (GPS). Some mobiles even allow you to watch television programmes.

Faster and freer

The speed of communications will continue to get faster in the future. Early internet connections were 'narrow-band' – they could only send information slowly (about 54,000 'bits' of information per second). Today's internet connections are broadband – they can send up to 8 million bits of information every second. The next generation of mobile phones (4G) will work at broadband speeds, while new internet connections will be over 12 times faster than current broadband speeds. In some countries, ultra-fast broadband

PCFs

Photonic crystal fibres (PCFs) could be the communications cables of the future. PCFs are made of silica glass, but instead of being solid, they have very tiny channels along their length. The channels filter out all frequencies of light except one, which is carried down the length of the fibre. This allows them to carry much more information than conventional optical fibres. PCFs can also be used to make an extremely bright kind of laser, called a sunlight laser. Sunlight lasers produce very brief pulses of light that are 10,000 times brighter than the sun. A laser this bright could be used to increase the amount of data carried by optical fibres.

links are already available. The future is also likely to be wireless. Already internet connections are available for laptop computers that work almost anywhere. In future this will become the norm rather than the exception.

A computer room, with free internet access, in Kenya. This computer room has been set up in Pumwani, a poor area, to help local people learn computer skills and take part in online training courses.

➕ PROS: FUTURE TECHNOLOGY

In the future, technology will make communications even simpler and more convenient than today. Combining several types of communication into one device will mean that people will not have to buy separate telephones, televisions, computers, radios, and so on. This will make keeping in touch even cheaper and more convenient.

➖ CONS: FUTURE TECHNOLOGY

Building good communications networks can be very expensive. It is hard for less developed countries to afford such communication networks. This difference in 'connectedness' between rich and poor countries has been called the 'digital divide'. Since 1999 the digital divide has narrowed a little. However, as more new technology is introduced, the divide could widen once more.

JEREMY BURROUGHES
Inventor

The future is plastic

A new technology that will change communications in the future is microchips made from polymers (plastics). This technology is already being used to make plastic electronic display screens that are thin, tough and flexible. If these screens can be made flexible enough to be rolled up or folded, a mobile with a roll-up screen could replace all our current communications devices.

It may not be long before another form of communication – printing – becomes obsolete. Instead people may read books, newspapers and

A test version of a television screen made using plastic electronics. The screen is only 2mm thick.

other documents electronically, using a digital reader. This is a device that can store printed material in its memory, and display them on a screen for reading. The latest digital readers use plastic electronics for their screens. It will not be long before these kinds of reader are flexible enough to be carried around as easily as a magazine or newspaper.

The internet in space

As part of its plans for space missions to the Moon and Mars, the US space agency NASA is developing an interplanetary communications network – a 'space internet'. At present, NASA technicians design a new communications system for each space mission they plan. But now they are working on a communications system that has the same basic rules for every space probe and satellite. Every spacecraft will eventually be part of a vast communications network spread out over space.

PROS: ELECTRONIC COMMUNICATIONS

The amount of information available to us through different media grows day by day. A very useful development for the future would be to find ways of filtering the information we receive, to avoid information overload. Intelligent computers might well be a way of doing this. They could search for information in a much more sophisticated way than today's search engines, and present only the most useful results.

CONS: ELECTRONIC COMMUNICATIONS

We already rely heavily on electronic communications, and in the future we will use them even more. But our reliance on electronics means that if they become damaged, there could be a complete communications blackout. This could cause huge disruption all over the world. Solar flares are one of the potential threats. A solar flare is like a massive explosion that blasts out clouds of electrically-charged particles, called a proton storm. A large flare can produce a proton storm that washes over Earth. The particles do not damage people or animals, but they can damage all kinds of electronics. The result of such a storm could be disastrous.

GLOSSARY

alloy A material formed from a mixture of metals.

amplifier An electronic device to boost an electrical signal (make it bigger or louder).

amplitude The height of a wave.

amplitude modulation (AM) A radio signal in which the carrier wave is modified by changing its amplitude.

analogue An electrical signal or wave that varies continuously.

bandwidth The amount of information that can be sent along a communications channel. A high-bandwidth channel can carry a lot of information.

binary number A number made up of only 0s and 1s. In binary code, one is 1, two is 10, three is 11, four is 100 and so on.

broadband A type of fast internet connection.

carrier wave A high-frequency radio wave that is used to carry information.

cell An area where mobile phones all connect to a particular transmitter.

charge-coupled device (CCD) A grid of light-sensitive detectors used to record images in a television camera.

circuit board A thin board with a number of electronic components on it.

compress To make smaller or more compact.

diaphragm In a microphone, a thin sheet of material that can vibrate.

digital An electrical signal or wave that varies in steps, rather than continuously.

dot-com company A business that buys and sells products and services via the internet.

electromagnetic radiation A whole range of similar waves or rays, including light, radio waves, microwaves, infrared, ultraviolet and X-rays.

electron A tiny, negatively-charged part of an atom. Electricity is a flow of electrons.

frequency The rate at which waves vibrate.

frequency modulation (FM) A radio signal in which the carrier wave is modified by changing its frequency.

geosynchronous orbit An orbit in which a satellite travels round the Earth at the same speed as the Earth spins. This means that the satellite seems to hover in the same spot in the sky when viewed from Earth.

global positioning system (GPS) A system of satellites circling above the Earth that are used for accurate navigation. Someone with a GPS handset can use information from the satellites to find their position almost anywhere on Earth.

grid computing A computing network that allows computers around the world to share not just information, but also programs and computing power.

hertz (Hz) A measure of frequency. One hertz is one cycle (vibration) per second.

GLOSSARY

high-definition television (HDTV) Television broadcasts with better-quality pictures than ordinary TV.

high-frequency Describes waves that vibrate back and forth very quickly (more than 3 million times per second).

hypertext Text containing words that have links to other related pieces of information.

integrated circuit An electronic circuit in which the transistors, diodes and other components are all fitted on to a single small 'chip' of semiconductor material.

internet service provider (ISP) A company that provides people with a connection to the internet.

liquid crystal display A type of flat-screen display containing materials called liquid crystals, which change properties when an electric current flows through them.

low-Earth orbit (LEO) An orbit less than 200km above the Earth's surface.

low-frequency Describes waves that vibrate back and forth relatively slowly (less than 300,000 times per second).

magnetic tape Plastic tape coated with a layer of tiny magnetic particles, which can be used to store recorded sound or video.

microchip An integrated circuit.

microprocessor A microchip that contains all the components of a central processing unit (the 'brains' of a computer).

microwaves Electromagnetic waves that have a higher frequency (more energy) than radio waves but a lower frequency (less energy) than infrared waves.

modulation When an electrical signal is used to modify (change) a carrier wave, so that the wave carries the information in the electrical signal.

Morse code A code in which letters are coded as a series of dots (short pulses) and dashes (longer pulses).

multiplexing Sending several messages at the same time along the same circuit or channel.

obsolete Describes something that is out of date and no longer used.

optical fibre A thin, flexible strand of glass that can be used to carry information as pulses of laser light.

outsourcing A practice used by some companies to reduce costs by basing parts of the business, call centres for example, in a country where rates of pay are significantly lower than in the home country of the company.

packet switching Sending messages as short 'packets' of information, which are put back together at their destination.

patent A grant awarded by a government that gives an inventor 'ownership' of his or her invention.

phosphor A chemical that gives out light when it is exposed to radiation.

GLOSSARY

pixel A picture element – a tiny dot or square of just one colour or shade, that forms part of an image.

plasma Very hot, electrically-charged gas.

radio valve An electronic device made from a glass tube containing one or more electrodes (wires carrying an electric current).

receiver A device that receives radio or other communications signals.

satellite An object that orbits a planet.

semaphore A signalling system in which letters and numbers are coded as positions of two 'arms' or flags.

semiconductor A material such as silicon or gallium, which is not a metal but can conduct electricity in certain circumstances.

server A powerful computer, or a program running on a computer, that offers services on the internet or another network.

signal Information carried by a varying electrical current or voltage, or by variations of a laser light beam.

silica glass A hard, clear, high-quality type of glass.

spectrum A range of different wavelengths of light or other electromagnetic radiation.

telecommunications Any system of communication at a distance.

telegraph A system of signalling using pulses of electricity along wires.

transceiver A combined transmitter and receiver.

transistor A semiconductor device that can act either as an amplifier or a switch.

transmitter A device that sends out radio or other communications signals.

type In printing, type is printed letters and numbers.

virus In computing, a program that can reproduce itself and is designed to corrupt or destroy information.

wavelength The distance between two peaks of a wave.

web browser A kind of computer software that allows people to look at text, images, videos, music, games and other information on internet websites.

FURTHER INFORMATION

WEBSITES

http://www.warriorsofthe.net/movie.html
Warriors of the Net. A great movie that you can download, explaining how 'packets' of information move about on the internet.

http://www.privateline.com/TelephoneHistory/History1.htm
Tom Farley's Telephone History. Everything you are ever likely to want to know about the telephone and its history.

http://www.mztv.com/
This is the website of the Museum of Television in Toronto, Canada.

http://distantwriting.co.uk/electrictelegraphcompany.aspx
The Electric Telegraph Company. An online history of the electric telegraph.

The FCC is the Federal Communications Commission, which regulates telecommunications in the United States. It has three interesting websites:

http://www.fcc.gov/cgb/kidszone/faqs_4.html
'Did You Know?' has simple explanations of things such as AM and FM radio, satellite technology and broadband on the internet.

http://www.fcc.gov/omd/history/tv/
Television Technology tells the story of the development of television.

http://www.fcc.gov/omd/history/radio/
Radio Pioneers is about the pioneers who first developed radio communications.

BOOKS

Constant Touch:
A Brief History of the Mobile Phone
John Agar, Icon Books (2003)

The Knowledge: Incredible Internet
Michael Cox, Scholastic (2002)

Scientists Who Made History:
John Logie Baird
Dr Mike Goldsmith, Hodder Wayland (2003)

Scientists Who Made History: Guglielmo Marconi
Dr Mike Goldsmith, Hodder Wayland (2003)

Communications Close-up: Radio and Television
Ian Graham, Evans Brothers (2003)

Internet Safety Skills
Ted Hastings, Leckie and Leckie (2007)

Navigators: Technology
Peter Kent, Kingfisher (2009)

Scientists Who Made History:
Alexander Graham Bell
Stewart Ross, Hodder Wayland (2001)

INDEX

Page numbers in **BOLD** refer to illustrations and charts.

AM (amplitude modulation) 20, **20**
amplifiers 12, 21, 54
analogue signals 14, 15, **15**, 36, 51, 54
Arctic Monkeys **45**
Armstrong, Edwin 20
ARPANET 38–9, 40

Baird, John Logie 28, 31
Bell, Alexander Graham 10, 11, **11**
Berners-Lee, Tim 42
binary code 14, 15, **15**
books 6, 59
broadband 56–7

call centres 17, **17**
carrier waves 19, 20, 22
cathode ray tubes (CRTs) 31, 36
Cerf, Vinton 39
Chappe, Claude and Ignace 7
cinema 30–1
communications satellites 8, 24–7, 34–5
computers 5, 15, 36, 38–47, 49, 50, 53, 56, **57**, 59

de Forest, Lee 20
digital divide 44, 57
digital radio 22, 23
digital readers 59
digital signals 14, 15, **15**, 36, 37, 54
digital television 36, 37
disc jockeys **23**
dot-com companies 44–5

eBay 44
Edison, Thomas 11, 12
electric telegraph 7, 8–10, **9**, 12, 14
electronic waste 55
emails 4, 40, 53, 55

Facebook 44
Farnsworth, Philo 28
Fessenden, Reginald 19
FM (frequency modulation) 20, **20**, 23
fraud 17, 40, 47

geosynchronous orbits 26
Global Positioning System (GPS) 53, 56
Google 5, 42, **43**, 44, **52**
Gray, Elisha 11
grid computing 46, **46**
Gutenberg, Johannes 6

Hertz, Heinrich 18
Hings, Donald 49
hypertext 42

INTELSAT 25
internet 4, 5, 6, 18, 22, 23, 34, 35, 38–47, **39**, **43**, 53, 56, **57**, 59
broadband 56
in space 59
instant messaging 40–41, **41**
radio 23
service providers 40, 42
wireless connection 46–7, 56–7

Licklider, Joseph 38
low-Earth orbits 26

Marconi, Guglielmo 18–19
microchips 15, 42, 54, 58
microwaves 25
mobile phones 26, 46, 48–55, **52**, **54**, 56
antennae 51
batteries 50, 54
cells 48, 49, 50, 55
components **54**, 54–5
dangers to health 53, 55
development 48–53
fourth generation (4G) 56
second generation (2G) 51
smartphones **52**, 53
texting 4, 18, 52
third generation (3G) 53
Morse code **8**, 8–9, 10, 18, 19
Morse, Samuel 8
Mosaic 42
multiplexing 16
MySpace 45

Nipkow, Paul 28

optical fibres 16, **16**

packet switching 38–9
patents **8**, 11
phototonic crystal fibres 56
printing 6, 58

radio 4, 5, 10, 16, 18–23, 24, 25, 28, 30, 31, 34, 46, 49, 54, 55, 56, 57
digital 22, 23

first broadcast 19
transmitter **19**
radio waves 18, 20, **20**, 22, 24, 25, 28, 34, 48, 54, 56
bandwidths 22
interference 21
spectrum 22, 24, 48
wavebands 22
Reeves, Alex 14–15
Ring, Douglas 48, 49
routers 38

satellites 8, **24**, 24–7, 34–5, 53, 59
orbits 26
semaphore 7, **7**
solar flares 59
space junk 26, 27
Strowger, Almon 13

TCP/IP 39
telemarketing 17
telephone 4–5, 10–17, **11**, **12** 18, 21, 25, **27**, 34, 40, 56
development 10–14
exchanges 13, **13**, 15
how it works 12
interference 14–15
long-distance calls 10, **11**, 16, 17, 24
satellite 27
television 4, 5, 22, 25, 26, 28–37, **29**, **30**, 45, 55, 56, 57, **58**
cable 34–5, 37
digital 36, 37
HDTV 37, **37**
recording 32–3
satellite **25**, 26, 34–5, 36
screens 31, **34**, 36, 37, **58**
text messaging 4, 18, 41, 52
Tomlinson, Ray 40
transistors 21, 50
triodes 20, 21

Vail, Alfred 8, 9
video 26, 32, 33, 36, 41, 47, 53, 55
Voyager 1 **5**

walkie-talkies 49, **49**
web browsers 42
Wheatstone, Charles 8
world wide web 42–3, 55

Young, Rae 48, 49